Thematic Units...

from The MAILBOX® magazine

FABULOUS FRIENDSHIPS

Even though your little ones seem fairly focused on themselves, their interest in others may be just about to blossom. Help youngsters discover the fabulous fun of friends with these activities and book suggestions about friendship.

ideas contributed by Marie E. Cecchini

FRIENDS DO THINGS TOGETHER.

THE GET-ALONG GAME
Children, like adults, usually have special friends they enjoy being with the most. If you'd like to encourage youngsters to play with different and perhaps new friends, introduce "The Get-Along Game." To play, group youngsters in pairs. Ask each pair to play together until they hear a signal such as a bell or a whistle. After an appropriate length of time, give the signal and ask youngsters to find a new partner. So long! It's time to get along!

MAKING MUSIC
Use musical instruments to demonstrate how some activities that are fun alone are even more fun with friends. One at a time, provide each child with an instrument. Ask the child to play his instrument alone; then direct him to let his instrument rest on the floor. When each child has had an opportunity to play his instrument alone, ask the children to play their instruments at the same time. Discuss the difference in the sound of the instruments when played alone and when played together. If desired take your young musicians outside and have a marching band parade!

WE GO TOGETHER
Gather a collection of items that go together—such as a vase and artificial flowers, a baseball and a bat, and a toy dog and a bone. Discuss the items that go together; then place the items in a box. Have each child close his eyes and take one item from the box. When each child has an object, ask him to find his partner by finding the person with the corresponding object. After playing the game, place the box of objects in a center for children to match independently.

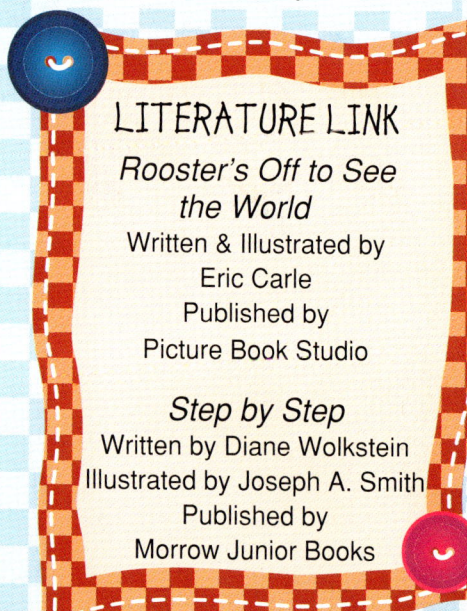

LITERATURE LINK

Rooster's Off to See the World
Written & Illustrated by
Eric Carle
Published by
Picture Book Studio

Step by Step
Written by Diane Wolkstein
Illustrated by Joseph A. Smith
Published by
Morrow Junior Books

Friendship

Preschool/Kindergarten

Table of Contents

Thematic Units

Fabulous Friendships..**4**
Help students discover how fabulous friends are with these nifty ideas!

A Celebration of Friendship **8**
Celebrate friends using the literature featured in this unit.

Building Character **12**
Use these ideas to teach virtues of cooperation and friendship.

More Activities and Ideas

More "Friend-ly" Ideas **15**
Look in this section for bulletin board ideas, group activities, songs, center ideas, and more. This selection of activities will provide your youngsters with a wealth of learning opportunities about friends!

Reproducible Activities

Friends **26**
Utilize Helme Heine's sweet story of friendship when completing these reproducible activities.

My Forest Friends **34**
Introduce your little ones to some forest friends and get them thinking about their own friends!

Friendship **42**
Invite your students to learn more about friends with these fun activities!

Save time and energy planning thematic units with this comprehensive resource. We've searched the 1990–1998 issues of **The MAILBOX®** and **Teacher's Helper®** magazines to find the best ideas for you to use when teaching a thematic unit about friendship. Included in this book are favorite units from the magazines, single ideas to extend a unit, and a variety of reproducible activities. Use these activities to develop your own complete unit or simply to enhance your current lesson plans. You're sure to find everything you need for strengthening student learning.

Project Managers: Sherri Lynn Kuntz, Scott Lyons
Copy Editors: Sylvan Allen, Gina Farago, Karen Brewer Grossman, Karen L. Huffman, Amy Kirtley-Hill, Debbie Shoffner
Cover Artist: Nick Greenwood, Kimberly Richard
Artist: Nick Greenwood
Typesetters: Lynette Dickerson, Mark Rainey

President, The Mailbox Book Company™: Joseph C. Bucci
Director of Book Planning and Development: Chris Poindexter
Book Development Managers: Stephen Levy, Elizabeth H. Lindsay, Thad McLaurin, Susan Walker
Curriculum Director: Karen P. Shelton
Traffic Manager: Lisa K. Pitts
Librarian: Dorothy C. McKinney
Editorial and Freelance Management: Karen A. Brudnak
Editorial Training: Irving P. Crump
Editorial Assistants: Terrie Head, Hope Rodgers, Jan E. Witcher

www.themailbox.com

©2002 by THE EDUCATION CENTER, INC.
All rights reserved.
ISBN# 1-56234-484-6

Except as provided for herein, no part of this publication may be reproduced or transmitted in any form or by any means, electronic or mechanical, including photocopying, recording, or storing in any information storage and retrieval system or electronic online bulletin board, without prior written permission from The Education Center, Inc. Permission is given to the original purchaser to reproduce patterns and reproducibles for individual classroom use only and not for resale or distribution. Reproduction for an entire school or school system is prohibited. Please direct written inquiries to The Education Center, Inc., P.O. Box 9753, Greensboro, NC 27429-0753. The Education Center®, *The Mailbox*®, *Teacher's Helper*®, the mailbox/post/grass logo, and The Mailbox Book Company™ are trademarks of The Education Center, Inc., and may be the subject of one or more federal trademark registrations. All other brand or product names are trademarks or registered trademarks of their respective companies.

Manufactured in the United States
10 9 8 7 6 5 4 3 2

FRIENDS ARE ALIKE AND DIFFERENT.

ALIKE AND DIFFERENT

Ask the children to describe their friends. Point out that some friends are very much alike while others are very different. Ask the children if they have friends who are older, younger, or perhaps are pets. Ask each child to draw a picture of an unusual friend with this unusual art technique. Provide the children with drawing chalk, colored paper, and a small bowl of milk. Direct each child to use the chalk to draw a picture of a friend who is very different from himself. To prevent smearing of the dried chalk, instruct the children to dip the tip of the chalk in the milk before drawing.

FRIENDSHIP GARDEN

By now your youngsters' social skills are probably blooming. This display is a beautiful way to show the diversity that exists in your classroom garden of friendship. Attach green, fringed paper to the bottom of a blue paper background. Provide children with various colors of construction paper and encourage them to cut out flowers, stems, and leaves. Have each child glue her flower parts together; then attach a photo of the child to the center of the flower. Mount the flowers onto the background along with the title "Our Friendship Garden."

LITERATURE LINK

Do You Want to Be My Friend?
Written & Illustrated by Eric Carle
Published by
HarperCollins Children's Books

My Friends
Written & Illustrated by Taro Gomi
Published by
Chronicle Books

FRIENDS HELP EACH OTHER.

OPERATION COOPERATION

During cleanup time, Operation Cooperation will really get the job done! Display a different-colored paper circle in each center or area of your room. Cut two smaller circles to correspond with the circle in each center. Store the smaller circles in a container. When cleanup time arrives, have each child select a circle from the container. Then pair students with matching circles and request that they work together to clean the corresponding center. Need to clean? Work as a team!

PASS-ALONG PICTURE

This *artwork* promotes *teamwork*. Seat a group of children in a circle on the floor. Provide each youngster with a marker or crayon. Select a child to draw on a large piece of paper. When he is satisfied with his work, have him pass the paper to the child seated next to him. When every child has had an opportunity to contribute, discuss the picture and how it might have looked different if one of the friends in the group had been missing. Before displaying the masterpiece, be sure to label it with the name of each child who participated in the group activity.

Shawna, Mackie, Britt, Sarah

LITERATURE LINKS

A House for Hermit Crab
Written & Illustrated by Eric Carle
Published by
Picture Book Studio

Fish Is Fish
Written & Illustrated by Leo Lionni
Published by
Pantheon

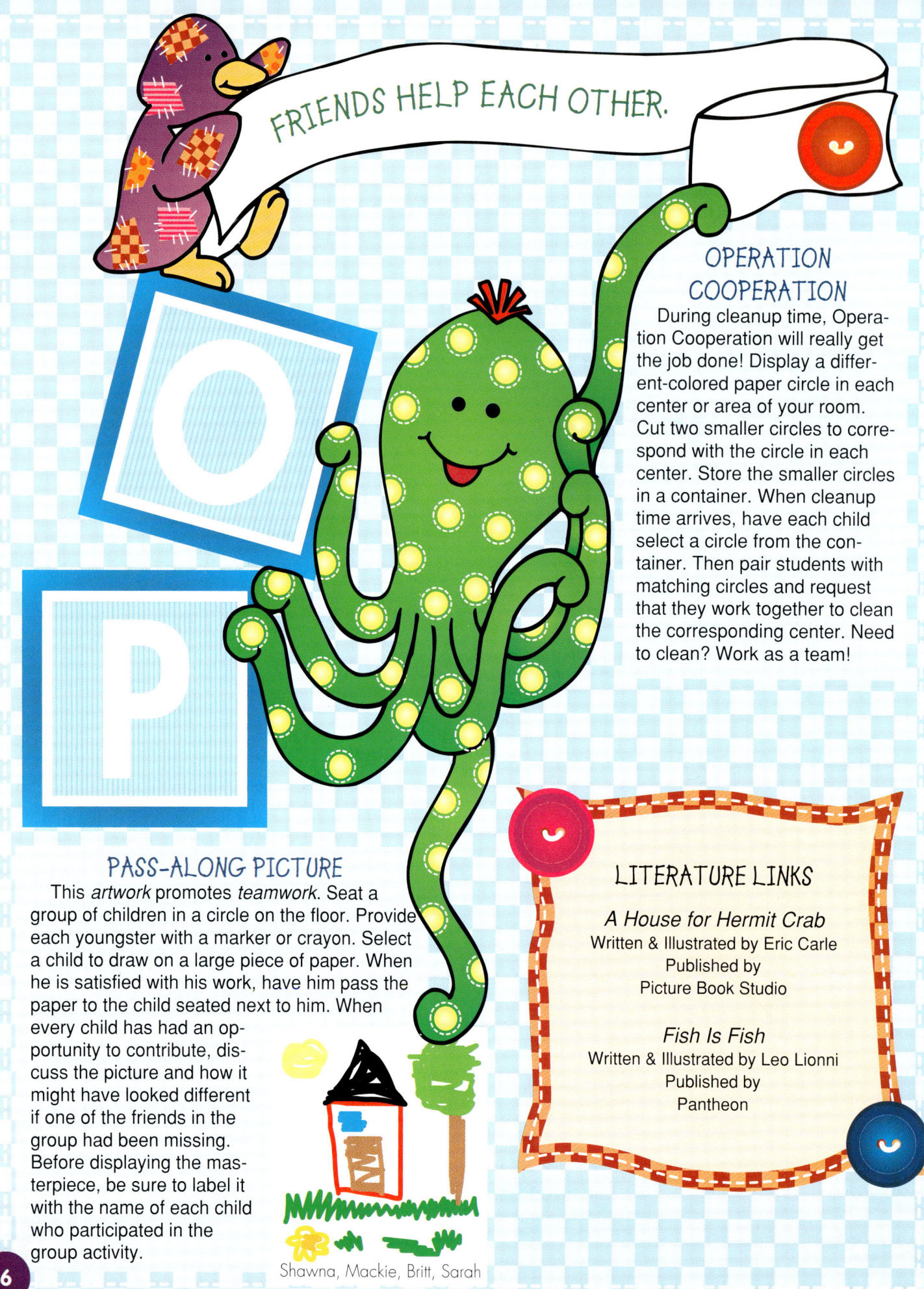

FRIENDS LIKE EACH OTHER.

FRIENDLY PHONE CALLS

Ring! Ring! Hello? Stay on the line for a fun idea. Collect phones from thrift shops or yard sales. Place the phones in your classroom housekeeping center. During a group time, discuss with youngsters proper use of the telephone. During the discussion, remind them to always ask an adult for permission to use the phone. Then encourage youngsters to practice what they have learned by "calling" each other when they visit the housekeeping center. Consider sending a note home to parents making them aware of this life-skills lesson.

IT'S PARTY TIME!

Celebrate your unit on friendship with a party. If desired have the children plan to invite another class to join them. Ask the children to decorate with stickers and glitter a supply of folded, construction-paper invitations. As a class plan and prepare the party refreshments. When the guests arrive, encourage the children to provide each guest with a plate of the prepared goodies. Later play a group game or organize a group activity such as mural painting. At the close of the celebration, be sure to remind the hosts to thank their guests for coming!

LITERATURE LINK

The Very Quiet Cricket
Written & Illustrated by Eric Carle
Published by
Philomel Books

A Celebration of Friendship

My Friends
Written & Illustrated by Taro Gomi
Published by Chronicle Books

A young girl recalls all that she has learned from her animal and people friends. Youngsters will enjoy the simple text and vibrant illustrations of Taro Gomi's charming book.

There is something to be learned from everything in the world around us. Help youngsters understand this idea by making a class book similar to the book *My Friends*. Brainstorm a list of animals; then talk about different actions or characteristics of each animal. For example, a fish swims and a lion roars. Ask each student to choose an animal to illustrate; then have him write (or dictate for you to write) a sentence about what he could learn from that animal. Bind the pages together with a cover. Title the book "Our Friends." Give each child an opportunity to take the book home for a night to share with his family.

Lisa Kranz—Gr. K
St. Ann School
Lansing, IL

Will I Have a Friend?
Written by Miriam Cohen
Illustrated by Lillian Hoban
Published by Macmillan Publishing Co., Inc.

Youngsters will identify with Jim's feelings as he spends his first day at school.

Use this reassuring story as a springboard for discussion about youngsters' feelings during the first days of school. Ask students to predict whether or not Jim will have a friend and if so, how Jim will meet his friend. After reading the book aloud, discuss the idea that everyone can be a friend to someone else in the class. On a chart, write several positive traits about each child that would make him a good friend. Then provide each child with a crown or an award ribbon cut from sturdy paper. Have each child personalize and decorate his item. Then write several positive words from the list on each child's crown or award.

Debbie Musser—Gr. K
Washington-Lee Elementary
Bristol, VA

The Rainbow Fish
Written & Illustrated by Marcus Pfister
Published by North-South Books

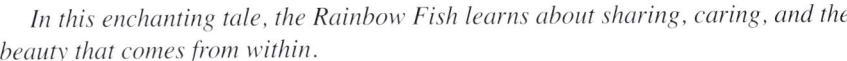

In this enchanting tale, the Rainbow Fish learns about sharing, caring, and the beauty that comes from within.

After reading the story aloud, discuss the importance of sharing in friendship. Then assist each child in making a Rainbow Fish book about sharing. To make a book, have each child cut two fish shapes (identical in size) from construction paper. Title one of the fish shapes "Sharing and Caring." Encourage the student to decorate this fish shape with paint, crayons, or markers. Using glitter and glue, have her make one shimmering scale on this fish. Place several sheets of paper (also cut in fish shapes) between the construction-paper fish, and bind them together to create a book. On each page, have the child illustrate and write (or dictate) ways that she can share and care.

Laurie Walegir—Gr. K
Twin Oaks Country Day School
Freeport, NY

Extend the beauty of this story by creating Rainbow Fish. Have each child paint rows of different colors on his own sheet of white art paper. After the paint dries, direct him to trace a fish pattern onto the paper and cut on the resulting outline. Onto the fish shape, glue a hole reinforcement for an eye and a small piece of tinfoil to represent the shimmering scale. Display the finished projects on a wall or bulletin board for a beautiful school of Rainbow Fish.

Barb Spero—Gr. K
Memorial School
Paramus, NJ

We Are Best Friends
Written & Illustrated by Aliki
Published by Greenwillow Books

Peter and Robert are best friends. Then Peter moves away. The two boys keep their friendship alive, however, by drawing pictures and writing letters to each other.

Before reading the story aloud, show students the front cover and read the title. On a chart, create a list of things that good friends do together. Explain that in the story one of the boys moves away. Provide an opportunity for children who have moved, or have had a friend who moved, to share their stories. Ask students to predict whether or not the two boys will stay friends. Read *We Are Best Friends* aloud. As an extension to the story, provide an opportunity for youngsters in the class to write letters to each other. Begin by having students play together in pairs outside or in centers. Then announce that it is "time to move." Ask students to sit at separate tables from their partners. Have each child illustrate what he did with his partner. Then demonstrate how to write a letter by starting with the word "Dear" and ending with the writer's name. Have each student write (or dictate) a letter to his partner. Use the class mail center, if available, to mail the letters.

Do You Want to Be My Friend?
Written & Illustrated by Eric Carle
Published by Philomel Books

Travel along with a brave, little mouse as he seeks to find a friend. You'll discover a mystery and a few surprises along the way.

After sharing the story, make friendship necklaces. Provide each child with a length of string or ribbon that has been taped on one end. Write each child's name on the tape at the end of his string. Also give each child a supply of beads equal to the number of children in the class. (Wooden beads from a beaded carseat mat work nicely for this. For an added touch of fun, paint the beads green so that the necklaces will resemble the surprise character at the conclusion of the story.) Direct each child to go to each child in the class and ask the question, "Do you want to be my friend?" As each child answers, "Yes," he should give one of his beads to the child asking the question. As children receive beads, they can accept these tokens of friendship and thread them on their strings. After each child has completed his friendship necklace, allow each student to trade necklaces with someone with whom he would like to be better friends. To ensure fairness in this necklace exchange, consider drawing names or pairing children appropriately.

Adapted from an idea by Jody Weber and
Sheila Dozark—Gr. K
Boyer Valley Community School
Dunlap, IA

We Are All Alike…We Are All Different
Written & Illustrated by the Cheltenham Elementary School Kindergartners
Published by Scholastic Inc.

Use this book written by children, for children, to foster in youngsters the appreciation of similarities and differences among themselves.

As children learn to understand human diversity, they grow in self-esteem and acceptance of others. To help youngsters better understand diversity, try this activity. Pair students. Give each pair a piece of paper that has been folded in half. Unfold the page. Have each child take a good look at his partner and then draw his partner on one half of the page. Have the students write (or dictate for you to write) one way that they are alike and one way that they are different.

Extend the learning opportunities of this child-centered book with an art activity. Using skin-toned construction paper, cut out a body shape for each student. Also cut out a supply of large, red construction-paper hearts. Encourage each child to decorate his body shape using a variety of art supplies such as fabric, yarn, and markers. Have each child write his name on a heart cutout and glue the heart to the right hand of the decorated cutout. Attach the completed projects side by side along a wall or on a bulletin board. For a display that clearly communicates the message of friendship in a diverse world, cut out a globe design and attach it to a bulletin board. Then add the bodies and hearts around the globe design. Title the display "We are all alike. We are all different. We are all friends."

Beth Lemke
Coon Rapids, MN

Bein' With You This Way
Written by W. Nikola-Lisa
Illustrated by Michael Bryant
Published by Lee & Low Books, Inc.

An African-American girl gathers a group of friends together for an afternoon in the park. The irresistible beat of this playground rap will have youngsters eager to join in. "So are you ready? All right! Here we go…."

This award-winning book is an excellent choice for introducing little ones to racial and physical differences. Read aloud *Bein' With You This Way*; then create a class version of the book. Write each page of the book's text on a separate sheet of construction paper. Title another sheet "Bein' With You This Way" to use as the cover. Then, on a warm, sunny day, take the class to the playground or on a field trip to a park. To capture the joy of "just bein' together," take candid photos of the children as they play. After the pictures have been developed, glue several of them around the text on each page in the class book. Laminate the covers and the pages of the book; then bind them together. Give each child an opportunity to take the book home to share with his family.

Jamaica's Find
Written by Juanita Havill
Illustrated by Anne Sibley O'Brien
Published by Houghton Mifflin Company

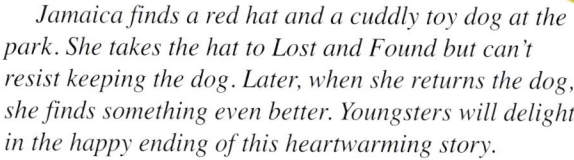

Jamaica finds a red hat and a cuddly toy dog at the park. She takes the hat to Lost and Found but can't resist keeping the dog. Later, when she returns the dog, she finds something even better. Youngsters will delight in the happy ending of this heartwarming story.

Read *Jamaica's Find* to the class; then have some fun with this secretive game of Lost and Found. Ask each child to bring a stuffed toy to school. Send a letter home to parents explaining the purpose of this activity and requesting that the toy be sent to school in a bag with the child's name attached. When it is time to play the game, collect everyone's bag; then redistribute the bags—giving each child a bag other than her own. Select a child to describe what her "lost" toy looked like. The children should look in the bags they are holding to see if the toy inside matches the description of the lost toy. The child with the matching toy can then announce that the lost toy has been "found." Continue play until each child has had a turn to describe her stuffed toy to the group.

Friends
Written & Illustrated by Helme Heine
Published by Margaret K. McElderry Books

"Good friends always stick together." That's what Charlie Rooster, Johnny Mouse, and fat Percy, the pig, believe. Celebrate the joy of friendship with these carefree characters as you read this delightful book.

After sharing the book, discuss how the characters enjoyed each other's companionship as well as the tasks they accomplished together. Ask students to think about who their good friends are. Then have each child draw a picture of himself with his friends and write (or dictate) a sentence about his friends. If possible, take a picture of each child with his friends. Mount each developed picture, if taken, on the paper.

Diane E. Stark—Gr. K
Hawthorne Elementary
Kansas City, KS

Good friends *will* stick together with these circles of friendship. To make one, fold a square piece of paper in half diagonally to form a triangle. Fold the triangle in half again; then fold once more. To make sure you have folded the paper correctly, open the paper and look for eight sections. Refold the paper. Trace a child-shaped pattern (as shown) onto the folded paper. Keeping the paper folded, cut out the shape. Open the paper to find a circle of eight "friends" holding hands. Have each student decorate each child shape in his circle. Then ask him to write a friend's name on each shape or to dictate ideas about friendship to be written on each shape. Display the circles of friendship on a bulletin board titled "Good Friends Stick Together."

Jennifer Barton—Gr. K
Elizabeth Green School
Newington, CT

Jessica
Written & Illustrated by Kevin Henkes
Published by Scholastic Inc.

No one could see Jessica except Ruthie. "There is no Jessica," said Ruthie's parents. But there was.

Ruthie's imagination led to the discovery of her first friendship. After reading the story aloud, ask each student to think about what her imaginary friend would look like if she had one (and many probably do!). Brainstorm a list of things that could be done with an imaginary friend. Show youngsters the picture Ruthie painted of herself and Jessica at school. Discuss the reasons Ruthie painted the frowns on their faces and how she would paint the picture differently after she had met the real Jessica. Place the book in an art or painting center. Encourage each child who visits the center to paint a picture of herself and her imaginary friend. Have the student write her name and her imaginary friend's name on the paper.

Chrysanthemum
Written & Illustrated by Kevin Henkes
Published by Greenwillow Books

Chrysanthemum loves her name. However, when she goes to school, everyone giggles—and Chrysanthemum wilts. Then she meets her music teacher. Suddenly, Chrysanthemum blossoms.

The beginning of the year is the perfect time to read *Chrysanthemum*. After sharing the book, encourage discussion about each child's name. Ask children if they know why their parents chose their names. Count the number of letters in Chrysanthemum's name. Then help each child count the number of letters in his own first name. For each child, visually divide a sheet of paper into columns as shown (or use one-inch graph paper). Help each child write his name on the paper: one letter in each space. Group the names together based on the number of letters in each name. Then create a class graph. Reread the story later in the year and graph each child's last name in the same manner.

Barb Spero—Gr. K
Memorial School
Paramus, NJ

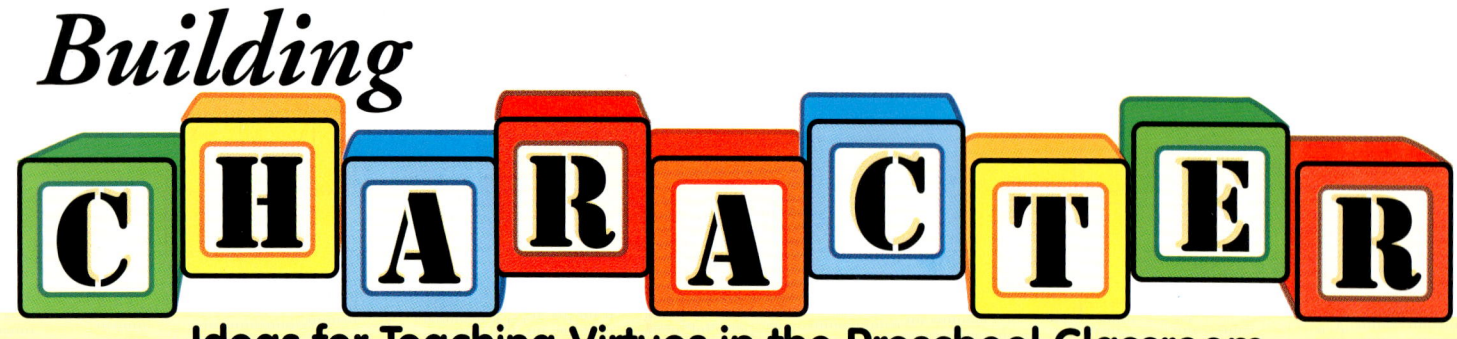

Ideas for Teaching Virtues in the Preschool Classroom
Friendship

by Lori Kent

Friends Do Things Together

Introduce your little ones to the virtue of friendship by reading aloud *Making Friends* by Fred Rogers (The Putnam & Grosset Group). Ask each student to tell something he likes to do with his classroom friends. List all responses on a sheet of chart paper. Have each child decorate a person shape to resemble himself. Display the shapes around the list on a bulletin board. Throughout the day, take pictures of friends playing together. Label each picture with the names of the friends shown; then mount them around the cutouts and chart.

Friends Work Together

Encourage cooperation skills with this group game that will have your youngsters island-hopping to a tropical beat. Prepare by cutting several large circles from bulletin-board paper to represent islands. Position the islands in an open area of your classroom. Invite students to pretend to swim around the islands as you play some tropical music. Stop the music; then have each child stand on an island. Count the number of children on each island. Remove one island and continue play. Each time the music stops, encourage children to work together to fit as many friends on an island as possible, being careful not to allow anyone to fall into the water. Words of encouragement and praise for cooperation skills will have all your little ones on friendly footing!

Friends Share

Follow up your island-hopping adventure with this refreshing activity. Lay the islands used in the previous activity on the floor of your classroom. Divide students into small groups; then have each group sit on an island. Provide each group with a plate with twice as many small snacks as there are people in the group. Have the students work together to divide the snacks evenly. Invite students to eat their snacks as they share a good time together.

Friendship

A Rainbow of Friends

Liken friendship to a rainbow—the combination of different colors creates a beautiful sight, just as the combination of different people can create wonderful friendships. Then invite children to create a rainbow. Set out red, yellow, and blue tempera paints. As a class, combine colors to create new colors until each color of the rainbow is represented. Have small groups each use a different color to sponge-paint a segment of a rainbow drawn on bulletin-board paper. (If desired, designate the color to be painted in each segment.) Afterward have each child create a self-portrait, paying careful attention to his color of hair, eyes, skin, etc. Display the rainbow with the title "A Rainbow of Friends." Then mount the self-portraits around the rainbow.

Susan Rushing—Gr. K, Metro Kids Care, Des Moines, IA

Photogenic Friendships

Capture those precious moments of friendship on film! Keep a camera in your classroom at all times; then take pictures of children as they spontaneously display qualities of friendship. Have the film developed in multiple prints; then mount a photo on a sheet of paper for each pictured child. Write that child's dictated statement about how or why the other pictured child (or children) is a friend. Encourage each child to take his friendship photo home to share. Both the student and his family will be pleased with the photogenic friendships that develop!

Gay Taylor—Pre-K, West Point Elementary, LaGrange, GA

Hugs to Give, Hugs to Get

Have you given and received your quota of hugs today? Four a day is the *minimum*, according to Charlotte Diamond's "Four Hugs A Day" on *10 Carrot Diamond* (Hug Bug Records). Discuss that hugging a friend is one way to show you care. Then share this lively, feel-good song that describes giving a hug (to order, call Educational Record Center at 1-888-372-4543). If you are unable to obtain the recording, have students say the rhyme below as they pass hugs to one another. Then invite youngsters to make this huggable project. Duplicate a class quantity of the hug pattern (page 14) on construction paper. Have each child decorate the head section to resemble himself. Then encourage students to show their friendship by giving hugs to—and receiving hugs from—one another. As a child receives a hug, have him request the hugger's signature on his pattern. Then show students how to fold the arms on their patterns so that they appear to be giving hugs.

**I have a hug. I give it to you.
Now you have a hug to give away, too!**

Hug Pattern Use with "Hugs to Give, Hugs to Get" on page 13.

©The Education Center, Inc. • *Friendship* • Preschool/Kindergarten • TEC3232

More "Friendly" Ideas

Friends Day

To promote interest and enrollment for the following year, we hold a Friends Day in our three- and four-year-old classes. Each child may bring a friend to school to show him or her the fun we have! During the day, we enjoy all of our favorite activities, such as easel painting, play dough, and the sandbox. We have found Friends Day to be a great enrollment booster.

Judy Meyer, Lakeshore Co-Op Nursery, St. Clair Shores, MI

Bake a Batch of Friendship!

Teaching cooperation and color mixing is a piece of cake with this unique idea! Use a mix to prepare white cake batter. Then fill a small cup with batter for each child. Invite each child to stir her choice of food coloring into her cup of batter; then have all the children pour their batter into a greased sheet-cake pan. After little ones have admired the cool color swirls, bake the cake according to the package directions. Once the cake has cooled, serve it with whipped topping and colored sprinkles. What a colorful and tasty treat!

Karen Sheheane—Preschool
United Methodist Preschool, Tallahassee, FL

Little Buddies

If your school has a preschool or if there is a preschool nearby, invite the youngsters in one of the classes to be "Little Buddies" to your kindergartners. Discuss with each of your students the responsibilities and importance of being a "Big Buddy." Then, throughout the year, arrange activities that both classes can do together. For example, have your students make a special snack and then share it with their buddies. Or invite the preschool class to join your kindergartners on a picnic. Your youngsters' self-esteem is sure to skyrocket with this opportunity to be "the bigger ones."

Karen Eiben
The Kids' Place, LaSalle, IL

We Love Our Friends

Help children recognize classmates' names with this heart-shaped game. Cut a sheet of red poster board into a large heart shape. Glue a photo of each child in your class onto the cutout. Label each picture with the child's name. Cut small hearts from colored construction paper and print a child's name on each one. Allow children to match the names and pictures.

Kathy Rollins—Three- and Four-Year-Olds
Children's Creative Corner
Springfield, MA

The Friendship Bottle

Cast a friendly spell of good behavior over your youngsters when using a magic friendship bottle. In advance, purchase a toy pendant that contains bubble solution and a wand to be the magic friendship bottle. Add a pinch of gold glitter to the bubble solution, if desired. Embellish the outside of the bottle with sequins, glitter, and colored foil. When a student exhibits friendly and cooperative behavior, give him the magic friendship bottle to wear. Then have him blow magic bubbles from the bottle to spread friendship throughout the classroom. During the course of the day, encourage the student wearing the pendant to choose another child who exhibits friendly behavior and place the pendant around his neck. This incentive is a great way to build self-esteem and camaraderie.

Margaret Lincoln—Gr. K
The Study
Westmount, Quebec, Canada

The Sharing Song

Use this song as a gentle reminder for kindergartners to share.

(sung to the tune of "Are You Sleeping?")

Are you sharing? Are you sharing?
Be a friend. Be a friend.
Sharing is caring. Caring is sharing.
Be a friend. Be a friend.

Amy Regan—Gr. K, Woodfern Elementary
Neshanic Station, NJ

Friendship Chain

Build friendship in your classroom by making this friendship chain. On the length of a sheet of construction paper, draw cutting lines two inches apart. (Prepare enough of these pages so that each child will be able to cut apart one strip.) Place the pages in an art center along with scissors and other art supplies. When a child visits this center, have him cut apart one strip, then sign it and decorate it as he likes. During a group time, have each child contribute his link to make a paper chain. As the child adds his link, ask him to share a way that he can be a good friend. Hang the finished project in your room to serve as a good friendship reminder.

Carmen Carpenter
Highland Preschool
Raleigh, NC

Here We Go Round the Friendship Circle

Whenever your youngsters are getting a little too active, use this method to help calm them down and refocus their attention. Begin to sing the tune that follows and motion for youngsters to sing along and form a circle. When everyone has joined your circle, sit and talk with youngsters a while before adjourning them to the next activity.

*(sung to the tune of
"Here We Go Round the Mulberry Bush")*

Here we go round the friendship circle,
  The friendship circle, the friendship circle.
Here we go round the friendship circle
  With our friends today.

Loretta McKeever—Preschool
ECCS Child Care Services
Norwood, NJ

Friends Share

Sharing is such an integral part of kindergarten, and here's a way to integrate some math into the concept. After reading books about sharing, such as *Friends* by Helme Heine (Aladdin Paperbacks) or *The Doorbell Rang* by Pat Hutchins (Mulberry Books), divide your students into small groups. Give each group a small bag of candy and the simple direction to share the candy fairly. Then watch the mathematical reasoning that takes place! Have students explain their solutions to you before they munch. Were there any extra pieces? Deciding what to do with that candy is also a problem-solving opportunity!

Deb Neumann—Gr. K, Clearwater Public, Clearwater, NE

To create this display, post a construction paper earth and the title. Have each child craft a person from skin-toned construction paper. Display the people around the earth as shown. From a basket of class names, have each child choose a classmate's name. Ask each child to write one good trait about the person he chose. Then have him cut out and glue his writing to a heart cutout. Display the hearts as shown.

adapted from an idea by Traci Schaffert, Hillcrest School, Morristown, NJ

Enlarge a set of friendly characters for this bulletin board, which encourages cooperation and friendship. Display the characters on a background. Then, as you see children working together, take an instant photo. On construction paper, write the students' description of their activity. Add the picture and the statement to the display. Friends work together!

Laura McDonough—Integrated Special Education Preschool, Brightwood Elementary School, Springfield, MA

Preschool Pals Pillowcase

Saying good-bye at the end of a year spent with friends can be difficult. Cheer up your little ones by having each child make a preschool pals pillowcase. Provide a white, prewashed pillowcase for each student, or ask each child to bring one. Inside each child's pillowcase, place a personalized sheet of paper that is the length and width of the pillowcase. On one side of each pillowcase, use a permanent fabric marker to write the poem shown, replacing the school name with your school's name. Then have each child use fabric paint to make a handprint on each pal's pillowcase. Label each handprint with the fabric marker. To permanently set the prints before washing, follow the paint manufacturer's instructions. When sleeping on these keepsakes, youngsters are sure to have sweet dreams of their preschool pals.

Cathy Schmidt—Preschool
DePere Co-op Nursery School, Green Bay, WI

Now I lay me down to sleep.
I'll count these hands instead of sheep
And always remember the friends I made
When I was at DePere Nursery School.

Friendship Song

Have youngsters sing this friendly melody while sitting in a circle holding hands.

(sung to the tune of "Jingle Bells")

Friends hold hands. Friends hold hands.
Friends hold hands and smile.
All our classmates are our friends.
Let's sing with them a while.

(Repeat entire verse.)

Betty Silkunas
Landsdale, PA

Friends From the Heart

Foster new friendships with this heartfelt idea. In advance, cut out a construction paper heart for each pair of students. Then puzzle-cut each heart differently to make two halves. (If you have an odd number of students, cut one heart into thirds.) Early in the day, have each child select a heart half. Then have him find the classmate who has the other half. Encourage each pair of children to work, play, and sit together throughout the day. You'll soon see youngsters getting to know each other better and becoming friends from the heart.

adapted from ideas by
   Sandie Sturgeon, Battle Ground, IN
Quazonia J. Quarles—Gr. K, Girls Inc., Newark, DE

Five Friends

Before introducing this song, write it on a sheet of chart paper, leaving blank spaces where the bracketed words are. Program sentence strips with number words from *zero* to *five*. Laminate the chart and the number cards. Attach Velcro® pieces to the number cards and the blank spaces. Then use a razor blade to cut five equally spaced slits at the bottom of the chart. Slide a paper clip into each of the slits. Next, make a classroom supply of the friend patterns on page 24. Cut the patterns out; then give one to each child. Encourage each child to decorate his friend pattern as he likes.

When you sing the song, choose five of the cutouts and attach them to the chart by sliding each one under a different paper clip. As you sing, have children remove the friends according to the lyrics. Repeat the verse, substituting the appropriate number words each time. When you get down to one friend, sing the last verse.

Tammy Riché—Gr. K, Kaplan Elementary, Maurice, LA

(sung to the tune of "Five Little Speckled Frogs")

[Five] friends went out to play
On a bright and sunny day,
Running and jumping all around. (Yeah! Yeah!)
One said, "I cannot stay. I must go home today."
Now there are [four] friends left to play.
OK!

(last verse)

One friend went out to play
On a bright and sunny day,
Running and jumping all around. (Yeah! Yeah!)
One said, "I cannot stay. I must go home today."
Now there are zero friends left to play.
Oh no!

Special People

Start a Special Person of the Week program with these super ideas. Select a different student each week to be the special person. Ask him to bring in some of his favorite items from home (such as photos, books, or games). After the student shows his favorite things to the class, display them on a table near a bulletin board. To decorate the bulletin board, cut balloon shapes from construction paper. Ask every student in the class to dictate a sentence about the special person. Write the comments on the balloons; then display them on the bulletin board. Give the balloons to the special student to take home when his week is over.

Linda Crosby—Gr. K
Hill Crest Community School
Fort Vermilion, Alberta
Canada

Teamwork is the secret ingredient that creates *and* solves this puzzle! To prepare, cut a large sheet of white poster board into as many pieces as you have children. Label each piece with the name of a different student. Then give each child her piece of the puzzle and invite her to decorate it as she likes. Ask each child to place her decorated piece on a large, flat surface in your puzzle center. During center times, encourage children to put the puzzle together—once, twice, or many times! Then mount the completed puzzle on a poster board frame.

Becky Krapf—Gr. K
Richard Mann Elementary School
Walworth, NY

The More We Get Together, the Happier We'll Be!

Friendship Friday

Since learning how to be a good friend is an ongoing process, try this ongoing activity. Put the individual names of all of your students in a hat. Each Friday select a child to choose a name from the hat. Have the chooser read the name that he chose. Then encourage the person whose name was selected to sit by the chooser. Continue in this manner until each child has a partner. (If the name of a child who already has a partner is chosen, select another name.) Throughout the day, encourage the pairs to do activities together, such as sitting together, playing together, and lining up together. At the end of the day, spend a few minutes talking about the day's events and friendship.

Terri Smith—Gr. K, Blessed Sacrament School, Trenton, NJ

Class Directory

A class directory is a super center idea that remains a favorite all year long. To make each directory page, mount a child's photograph on a large index card. Then (with parental approval) print each child's name, address, and telephone number on the card. Bind the pages together between two laminated construction paper covers. Place the class directory in a telephone, housekeeping, post-office, or letter-writing center.

Mary Lou Vogler—Gr. K
Port Monmouth Road School
Keansburg, NJ

Warm up to winter's chill with this friendly bulletin board. Cut two large mittens and arms from bulletin board paper. Staple the pieces to a bulletin board to resemble a pair of outstretched arms and cupped hands. Help each youngster fold and then cut out her own snowflake shape from white paper. Glue the child's photo to the center of her snowflake; then add the snowflake to the board. Finish by writing the title on the mittens as shown.

Elinor Gesink—Gr. K, Sheldon Christian School, Sheldon, IA

Celebrate students' differences, similarities, school experiences, and friendships with this visual treat. With bulletin board paper, create rolling hills and blue skies. Have each child cut out a skintone copy of the friend pattern (page 24) and then convert it into a self-portrait by selecting from a wide range of art supplies. Ask him to dictate something about his favorite things to do at school as you record his thoughts on a speech-balloon cutout. Positioning students' artwork at many different angles, attach each self-portrait to the board with the corresponding dictation. Now *that* will give 'em something to talk about!

Tarie Curtiss—Gr. K, Arthur Road Elementary School, Solon, OH

Friendship Train

Make a friendship train for an attractive room display. Have each child write his name on a sheet of construction paper and glue two circles onto the construction paper to resemble a boxcar. Mount the boxcars on a wall behind an engine cutout. Program the engine cutout with your name and grade. Connect the parts of the train using yarn. All aboard the friendship train!

Lisa Anne Totora—Gr. Pre/K
First United Methodist Church
New Orleans, LA

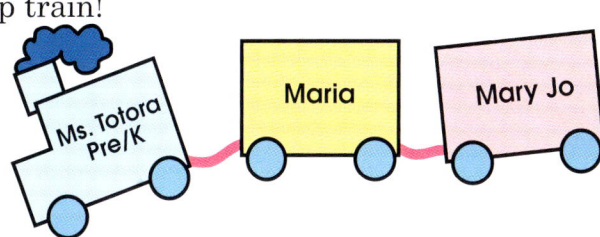

Friend Patterns
Use with "Five Friends" on page 20 and with the display on page 23.

Reproducible Activities...

from TEACHER'S HELPER® magazine

Friends

Note to the Teacher
This unit is designed to be used with *Friends* by Helme Heine.
After enjoying the story with your students, lead them in completing the related activities on pages 27–33.

Story Synopsis
Friends
This delightful story begins as three barnyard buddies start a busy day. They wake up the other farm animals, take their morning bicycle ride, play hide-and-seek, conquer the pond, fish, snack on cherries, and suffer through stomachaches—*together*. Throughout the day, the trio affirms several rules of friendship: always stick together, always decide things together, and always be fair. At the end of the day, the tired friends swear to remain friends forever and then plan to spend the night together. When they can't find a suitable place to sleep, the three pals decide that good friends can't *always* be together. But that doesn't stop them from dreaming of each other—"the way true friends do."

Illustrations by Helme Heine.
Reprinted by permission of Simon & Schuster.

Name _____

Friends
Characters

Farm Fellows

🖍 Color the animals seen in the story.
✏️ Circle the three good friends.

28 ©The Education Center, Inc. • *Friendship* • Preschool/Kindergarten • TEC3232

Name_____

Friends
Color words

Cock-a-Doodle-Doo Colors

Read.
🖍 Color.

- red
- green
- yellow
- red
- purple
- brown
- blue
- black
- orange
- orange

©The Education Center, Inc. • *Friendship* • Preschool/Kindergarten • TEC3232

Materials Needed for Each Student

9" x 12" piece of white construction paper
12" x 18" piece of green construction paper
2" x 6" strip of yellow construction paper
9" white paper plate
discarded catalogs of toys or sports equipment
crayons
scissors
glue
stapler

Finished Sample

How to Use Page 31

Duplicate page 31 onto the white construction paper for each child. Then have him complete the following directions, assisting when necessary:

1. Color and cut out the illustrations.
2. Color the paper plate blue to represent the pond in the story.
3. Staple or glue the sides and bottom of the boat to the middle of the plate to make a pocket. Then glue the mast to the plate so that it appears to be attached to the boat.
4. Staple or glue the plate to the right side of the piece of green paper.
5. Draw lines of green grass along the strip of yellow paper; then fringe-cut one side of the strip to resemble the grassy field in the story.
6. Staple or glue the sides and bottom of the fringed strip to the green paper to make a pocket.
7. Glue the cherry tree to the green paper.
8. Cut out a picture of a bicycle from a discarded catalog and glue it to the green paper.
9. Use crayons to draw any additional places or things from the story on the green paper.
10. Store the three story characters in the pockets.

Invite each child to retell the *Friends* story in his own words as he manipulates the characters on the background. The paper can be folded in half for easy transport home.

Name_____

Friends Craft

Playful Pals

🖍 Color.
✂ Cut.

How to Use Pages 32 and 33

1. Duplicate the pages for each child.
2. Go over the name for each of the pictures on this page.
3. Have each child cut out these pictures and glue them in the corresponding boxes on page 33.
4. Encourage more advanced students to label each picture using phonemic spelling.

Beginning-Sound Pictures

32

©The Education Center, Inc. • *Friendship* • Preschool/Kindergarten • TEC3232

Name_____

Friends
Beginning sounds

Friendly Phonics

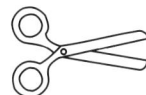 Cut.   Match.    Glue.

m

p

r

My Forest Friends

Note to the Teacher

This unit on friends and what friends do together can be made into, and used as, a booklet. To do so, duplicate pages 35, 37, 39, and 41 for each child. Staple the pages inside a construction paper cover. Duplicate the "My Forest Friends Book" cover cutout below for each child. Allow the children to color and cut out the forest friends and paste them to their booklet covers.

Oral Instructions for Page 35

1. *Read the four-line poem to the children and ask the following questions.*
2. What are the rabbit and the squirrel doing? *(working)*
3. What are they working to make? *(a pretty yard)*
4. What plants and other things might they put in their yard?
5. Draw and color what the rabbit and squirrel put in the yard.

Optional thinking questions for this page:
Have you ever worked with a friend?
What did you do?
How did it feel to work with a friend?
Why is it helpful to work with a friend?

Finished Sample

Book Cover

My Forest Friends Book

by _____

Name _____ Friends

Friends can work together
To finish something hard.
These friends can work together
To make a pretty yard.

Friends can work.

Oral Instructions for Page 37

1. *Read the four-line poem to the children and ask the following questions.*
2. What are the fox and bobcat doing? *(sitting, playing)*
3. How do they feel about playing together? *(happy)*
4. What toys might they be playing with?
5. Draw and color some toys for the friends to play with.

Optional thinking questions for this page:
    Why do you like to play with friends?
    Do friends *always* get along?
    What can you do to make up with a friend after you've had a fight?
    Why is it sometimes hard for friends to get along?
    Tell about a fun time you had with a friend.

Name _____

Friends _____

Friends can play together
When they want some fun.
Friends can play and share their toys
And clean up when they're done.

Friends can play.

Oral Instructions for Page 39

1. *Read the four-line poem to the children and ask the following questions.*
2. What are the raccoon and opossum doing? *(carrying a box)*
3. How are they helping each other? *(The box is too heavy for one.)*
4. What might be in the box?
5. Draw and color something in the box.

Optional thinking questions for this page:
    Have you ever helped a friend?
    What did you do?
    How did it feel to help a friend?
    Why should we help each other?
    Have you ever not wanted help to do something?
    What can you do if you don't want to help someone else?

Friends can help each other
With jobs too big for one.
A friend can help you with a job
And make it lots of fun.

Friends can help.

Oral Instructions for Page 41

1. *Read the four-line poem to the children and ask the following questions.*
2. What are all of the friends doing?
3. How do they feel about sharing?
4. What kinds of treats might they be sharing?
5. Draw and color some treats on the table.
6. *Allow the children to write (or dictate) about what the friends are sharing on the line provided.*

Optional thinking questions for this page:
> How do you feel when you share with someone?
> Why is it important to share?
> Have you ever shared a meal with friends?
> How does it feel to share a special time with friends?
> Have you ever not wanted to share?
> Is it all right not to share sometimes?

Name _____

Story starter

Friends can share together
When they want a treat.
These friends are sharing something
That's very good to eat!

The friends are sharing _____

Friendship

How to Use Page 43

1. Duplicate the page on construction paper for each child.
2. Have each child color her page.
3. Have each child personalize her journal cover.
4. Stack five to ten sheets of white paper between the decorated front cover and a construction paper back cover; then staple the journal.
5. On selected days, have each child use one page in her journal to record the date. Then encourage her to draw and/or write about experiences she has had with her friends.

Finished Sample

Name _____   Friendship/Sharing

How Can We Share?

Show how each group can share. ✏️ Draw.

My Friendship Goals

My name is

I can be a friend.

I can use **friendly words.**

I can **talk** about **problems.**

I can **take turns.**

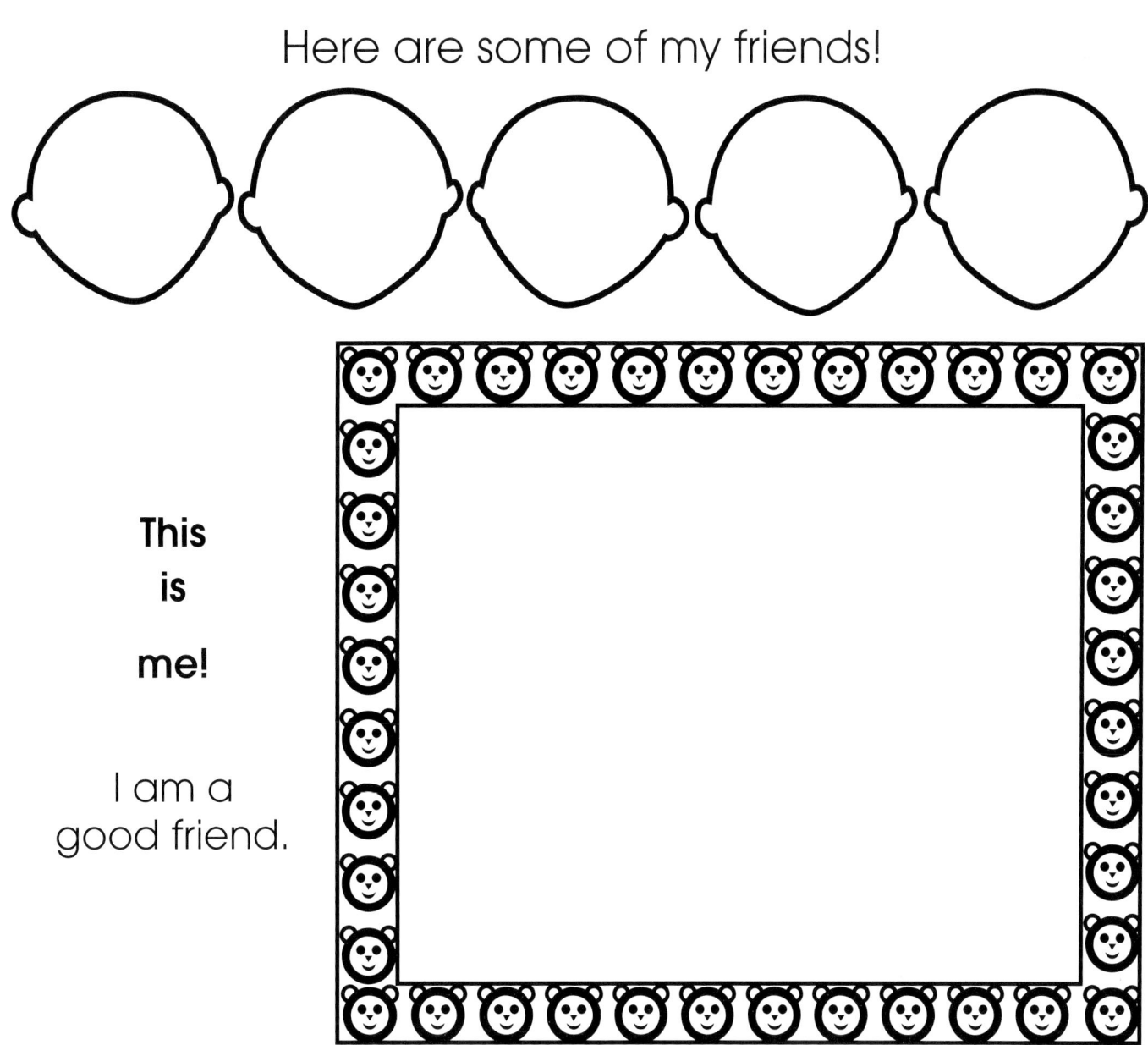

Here are some of my friends!

This is me!

I am a good friend.

How to Use Page 47

1. Use the pictures at the bottom of the sheet to begin discussion about what a friend is and how to be a friend. Discuss the positive concepts of sharing, playing, helping, having fun, and working. Also discuss the negative concepts of fighting, breaking each other's things, and stealing. Allow time for children to relate their own experiences. Be sure to include discussion about dealing with hurt feelings when friends fight or argue and how to be friends again after a disagreement.
2. The children should color the four pictures at the bottom of the page that show friends when they are getting along.
3. Tell the children to look at the top of the page. Tell the following story:

   A new boy at school is playing alone on the playground. He is smiling and waving at you. Trace and finish the drawing to show what your hand will do and how your face will look when you are friendly. Color the picture of the new friends.

Name_____ Thinking

Fun With Friends

 Think. Decide. ✏ Trace. 🖍 Color.

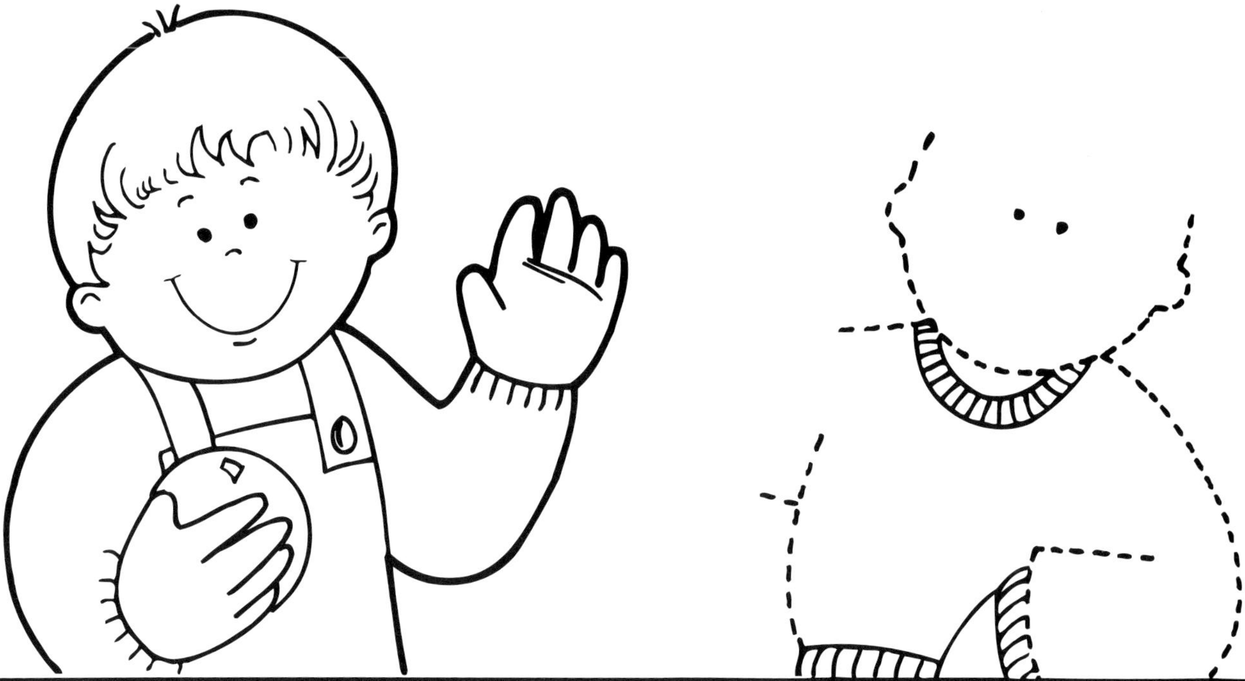

©The Education Center, Inc. • *Friendship* • Preschool/Kindergarten • TEC3232

47

Extension Activities
Friendship

— Bring a white, full-size bedsheet from home. Using a permanent marker, draw one large oval for each child around the perimeter of the sheet. Spread the sheet out on the floor. Have each child use bright-colored fabric paints to paint his self-portrait in one of the ovals. Once the fabric is dry, write your name, grade level, and room number in the center of the sheet. Then have your youngsters use fabric paints to make handprints on the sheet next to their self-portraits. This friendship sheet makes a great display in any classroom.

— Display the many patches of friendship in your classroom by making a friendship quilt. To make a quilt, cut several rectangles of different colors of brightly colored construction paper. Give each child one of the rectangles. Have him glue a photograph of himself in the middle of the rectangle. Instruct each child to decorate the remainder of the rectangle with yarn, beads, sequins, and glitter. Finally, staple the rectangles, side by side, on a bulletin board to create a paper friendship quilt.

Finished Sample